Published by UK Book Publishing

www.ukbookpublishing.com

ISBN: 978-1-916572-93-5

Introduction

Money Matters: A Teen's Guide to Financial Freedom is an informative and engaging guidebook that empowers teenagers to take control of their finances and build a strong financial foundation for their future. The book covers a range of topics, including banking basics, budgeting, saving and investing, and earning money through part-time jobs and entrepreneurship.

Written in a clear and accessible style, Money Matters provides practical tips and real-life examples to help teenagers understand the importance of managing money wisely. The book also emphasizes the value of delayed gratification, patience, and self-control when it comes to achieving financial goals.

At the end of each chapter, there's an exercise for you to practice and take notes about that chapter, this is to keep the mind active by engagement.

Whether you're a teen looking to learn more about money management or a parent or educator seeking a resource to help young people develop financial literacy, Money Matters is an invaluable guide to achieving financial freedom and success.

Table of contents

Chapter 1: Earning Money

Earning money is the process of exchanging your time and skills for compensation. This can come in the form of cash, checks, or other forms of payment, and can be earned through various means such as part-time jobs, freelance work, or entrepreneurship.

When you earn money, you are essentially providing a service or completing a task for someone else, and they are compensating you for your effort. For example, if you work part-time at a restaurant, you are providing a service by taking orders, preparing food, and serving customers. In exchange for your time and effort, the restaurant will pay you a predetermined amount of money.

Earning money is an important aspect of financial independence, as it allows you to save and invest for your future, as well as to pay for your current needs and wants. It is also a valuable opportunity to gain work experience and develop important skills such as time management, communication, and problem-solving.

Overall, earning money is a critical part of managing your finances and achieving your financial goals. Whether you choose to earn money through a part-time job, freelance work, or entrepreneurship, it is important to understand the value of your time and skills and to use them in a way that benefits both yourself and others.

Now let's look at the different ways teenagers can make money.

Babysitting: Many parents are willing to pay a responsible and trustworthy teenager to look after their children while they go out for the evening or for a date night. Babysitting can be a great way to earn extra cash on weekends or during school holidays.

Babysitting can be an excellent opportunity for teenagers to earn some extra money while also gaining valuable experience in responsible childcare. As a babysitter, teenagers may be responsible for feeding and entertaining children, helping with homework, and putting them to bed. In addition to earning money, babysitting can also help teens develop their communication, problem-solving, and decision-making skills.

Yard work: Teenagers can offer their services for lawn mowing, weed pulling, or other outdoor chores for neighbors or family friends. It's a great way to earn money while getting some fresh air and exercise.

To get started with yard work, teenagers can begin by advertising their services in their local community through flyers, word of mouth, or social media. There are also opportunities for teenagers to specialize in certain types of outdoor work, such as landscaping or gardening, therefore offering more specialized services and potentially earn higher pay rates.

Pet care: Some people are willing to pay for help with their pets. This could include dog walking, pet feeding, or even pet sitting while the owner is away on vacation. If you are an animal lover, this could be a great way to earn money doing something you enjoy.

Dog walking is a popular service that can be very lucrative. Many busy pet owners don't have time to walk their dogs as often as they would like, so they may be willing to pay for someone to take their dog for a walk during the day. You can charge by the hour or by the number of dogs you walk, and you can even offer special services like off-leash hikes or dog park outings.

Freelance work: Teens can also offer their skills for hire. For example, if you have good writing skills, you could offer to write blog posts or articles for websites. If you are good with computers, you could offer to help people with computer-related tasks such as setting up websites or troubleshooting issues. Many teens have good artistic skills in areas of painting, drawing, performance, modeling etc.

Another freelance job worth considering is content creation. Recent technological has made it possible and even easy for content creation. This is where you create engaging contents online for users and viewers, thereby creating a following which leads to income generation.

Part-time job: A part-time job is a classic way for teens to earn money. Many restaurants, retail stores, and other businesses are often looking for part-time workers, especially during busy seasons. Working part-time not only provides a steady income, but also valuable work experience that can help build your resume for future jobs.

Working part-time can also help teenagers learn important life skills, such as time management, responsibility, and teamwork. They will need to manage their time effectively to balance school work and their job responsibilities, which can be a great way to develop time-management skills. They will also need to be responsible and show up to work on time, which can help them develop a strong work ethic.

Exercises

1. What are five different ways you can earn money as a teenager?

2. Why is it important to have a good work ethic and do your best when earning money?

3. How can earning money help you develop valuable skills and gain work experience?

4. What are some potential challenges you may face when trying to earn money, and how can you overcome them?

5. What are some long-term financial goals you can work towards with the money you earn?

Chapter 2: Banking, Saving & Investing

Banking is the next important part of managing your money, and it all starts with understanding the basics. One of the first things you'll need to learn is how to open and manage a bank account. There are two main types of accounts you'll want to know about: savings accounts and checking or current accounts.

The concept of bank accounts

A savings account is a type of account where you can store your money and earn interest on it. Interest is like a small bonus that the bank pays you for keeping your money with them. A savings account is a low-risk way to save your money and watch it grow.

A checking or current account, on the other hand, is an account that you can use to pay bills and make purchases using a debit card or cheque. These accounts are more flexible for everyday transactions but may have lower interest rates.

Once you have a bank account, it's important to know how to manage it properly. This means keeping track of your transactions, balancing your checkbook, and making sure you don't overdraft your account. Overdrafting means spending more money than you have in your account, which can result in costly fees and other problems. You'll also want to know how to use online banking and mobile apps to monitor your account, and make transactions.

Some banks also offer overdraft protection, which can help you avoid fees if you accidentally overdraw your account. However, overdraft protection can come with its own fees, so it's important to understand how it works before signing up for it.

Saving

Let's talk about saving, which is an essential component of wise money management. Saving refers to holding onto a portion of your money rather than using it all up immediately. It's like sowing financial future-oriented seeds!

Saving is crucial for a number of reasons. You can first create an emergency fund thanks to it. Because of the unpredictability of life, unforeseen costs like medical expenses or auto repairs may appear. Saving money can act as a safety net and provide you peace of mind because you will always have a buffer to fall back on.

Second, saving can help you in reaching your financial objectives. Regularly setting money aside can help you achieve your goals faster, whether they are short-term objectives like college or establishing a business, or long-term ones like a dream vacation or new device. Seeing your funds increase and realising you're getting closer to your goals is exhilarating.

Saving also aids in the development of sound financial practises and the ability to resist gratification. To avoid the allure of impulsive purchases and instant gratification is not always simple. By saving, you're teaching your patience and how to put long-term happiness above instant gratification. Having control over your finances and the ability to deliberate about how you want to utilise them is also empowering.

You can make a budget with a savings category and put up specific saving goals to get started saving. Make it a habit to save the amount you have decided to each month before you spend it on other things. If you want to deposit your money and watch it increase over time with the help of interest, think about opening a savings account with a bank. Some financial institutions even provide accounts just for teenagers!

Investing

Another option is to invest your money in stocks, bonds, or mutual funds. Investing can be more risky than saving because the value of your investments can fluctuate based on market conditions. However, it also has the potential for higher returns over the long term. It's important to do your research and consult with a financial advisor or a trusted adult before investing your money in the stock market.

One key aspect of managing a bank account is to regularly monitor your account balance and transactions, either by reviewing your account statement or by checking your account online or through a mobile app. You'll also want to make sure to keep your account information secure, such as by using a strong password and not sharing your account information with anyone else.

A cryptocurrency is a digital form of currency that uses cryptography for security and operates independently of a central bank. Investing in cryptocurrency involves purchasing digital coins or tokens in the hope that their value will increase over time. While it can be exciting to invest in this new technology, it is important to remember that cryptocurrencies can be very volatile and risky investments. It's essential to research and understand the risks involved before investing any money. Additionally, it's important to be aware of the various cryptocurrencies available and their differences, as well as the different ways to purchase and store them securely.

A third option for young teenagers is to save money in a college savings plan, such as a trust or 529 plan. A trust is a tax-advantaged savings plan designed to help families save for college expenses. By contributing to a trust plan, you can potentially save money on taxes and earn interest on your savings.

It's important to remember that saving and investing require patience and discipline. You may not see significant returns on your investments right away, but over time, they can grow substantially. It's also important to set clear financial goals and create a plan for achieving them. By starting to save and invest early in life, you can set yourself up for a more secure financial future.

One way to create a savings plan is to figure out how much money you need to save and how long it will take you to save that amount. For example, if you want to save $20 for a new toy and you get $5 a week in allowance of job, it will take you four weeks to save up enough money. There's more about this we will cover in another chapter.

Keeping this in mind, saving and investing still allows you to enjoy your money right now. However, finding a balance between spending, saving, and investing is important. You'll be able to pursue your aspirations and deal with unforeseen circumstances with confidence if you save sensibly. In order to see your savings grow like a tree that will provide shade and security for your financial path, start saving early and make it a habit.

Exercises

1. What is the difference between a savings account and a checking account?
2. Why is it important to have a bank account and manage your money effectively?
3. How can you start saving money and what are some strategies to help you save regularly?
4. What are some basic investment options available to teenagers, and why is investing important for long-term financial growth?
5. How can you make informed decisions when choosing a bank or financial institution to open an account with?

Chapter 3: Spending Money

As a teenager, you have a lot of options for how you can spend your money. Some of the most common things you might choose to spend your money on include clothing, entertainment, food, and transportation. Clothing can be a significant expense for many teenagers, as keeping up with the latest fashion trends can be important for social reasons. You might choose to spend your money on new clothes, shoes, or accessories to help you feel confident and stylish.

Entertainment is another common area where teenagers choose to spend their money. This might include going to the movies, attending concerts or sporting events, or playing video games. Many teenagers also enjoy spending time with friends, which can involve going out to eat, bowling, or doing other fun activities together.

Food is a necessity, but it can also be a significant expense for many teenagers. You might choose to spend your money on eating out at restaurants, buying snacks or drinks at the mall or movie theater, or purchasing food to prepare at home. Transportation is another area where teenagers might spend money, whether that means paying for gas for your car, buying a bus pass, or taking an Uber or Lyft ride.

Many teenagers save up their money to travel, either with friends or family. Whether it's a road trip, a beach vacation, or an international adventure, travel can be a great way to experience new cultures and create lifelong memories.

It's important to remember that when you spend money, you are making choices about how to allocate your resources. It's easy to get carried away and spend more than you can afford, but developing good spending habits early on can help you make wise financial decisions in the future. When we spend our money, it's also important to think about how much things cost. Some things are more expensive than others, and we need to make sure we have enough money to buy everything we need and want. We can also look for good deals and sales to help us save money. By prioritizing your spending and making intentional choices about where you put your money, you can learn to manage your finances effectively and achieve your financial goals.

Difference between needs and wants

As a modern-day teenager, it's important to understand the difference between needs and wants when it comes to spending money. Needs are things that are necessary for survival, such as food, shelter, clothing, and healthcare. Wants, on the other hand, are things that are not necessary for survival but may enhance our lives or bring us enjoyment, such as video games, concert tickets, or the latest fashion trend.

It's important to prioritize your spending on needs before wants, as fulfilling your basic needs should always come first. For example, if you have limited money available, it's more important to spend it on groceries or rent than on buying a new video game. However, it's also okay to treat yourself to some wants, as long as you have enough money to cover your needs and other important expenses like savings or investments.

Learning to distinguish between needs and wants can help you make better financial decisions, and avoid overspending on things that aren't truly necessary. By prioritizing your spending based on your needs, and setting aside money for your wants, you can develop healthy spending habits and achieve financial stability in the long run.

Making good spending choices

Making good spending choices as a teenager is important because it can have long-term effects on our financial well-being. If we consistently spend all of our money on non-essential items, we may find ourselves struggling to cover necessary expenses in the future. But if we prioritize our needs, make choices based on our goals and values, and develop good saving habits, we'll be setting ourselves up for a more stable and successful financial future.

Another aspect of making good choices about spending is considering the value and quality of the things you're buying. It's easy to get caught up in trends or peer pressure and spend money on things that may not bring lasting satisfaction. Instead, take the time to research and compare products or services to ensure you're getting the best value for your money. Think about whether the item or experience will truly enhance your life and bring you long-term happiness.

Showing discipline towards money spending means you are mindful of their financial situation and make informed decisions. You consider the value and durability of your purchases, comparing prices and seeking the best deals. You also recognize the importance of saving and investing for the future, setting aside a portion of your income instead of spending it all. By doing so, you can build a sense of financial security and plan for your aspirations, such as saving for college or a desired purchase like an apartment for when you start living on your own.

Exercises

1. What is the difference between needs and wants? Provide examples of each.
2. Why is it important to make good choices when spending your money?
3. How can you prioritize your spending and make sure you have enough money for both your needs and wants?
4. What are some strategies you can use to avoid impulsive buying and save money for the things that are most important to you?
5. How can you practice responsible spending and make sure you are getting the best value for your money?

Chapter 4: Expenses & Budgeting

Expenses are simply what you spend money on. As a result of earning money, obligations arise. Part of which is the importance to manage your money carefully as well as spend it. You must decide how best to distribute your income after taking into account your requirements and desires. Consider your priorities and ambitions in this regard. For instance, if you're putting money aside for a certain thing or event, you might decide to allocate.

Understanding your expenses is essential to managing your revenue. This is being aware of your spending patterns and watching how much you spend. To make sure you have enough money to pay for your needs, such as food, transportation, and school supplies, while also being able to indulge in some of your wants, it's critical to budget for and keep track of your spending.

When making purchases, practice smart shopping techniques. Compare prices, look for sales or discounts, and consider buying secondhand or used items when appropriate. Avoid impulse buying and take the time to research products or services before making a decision. Additionally, be cautious of marketing tactics that try to persuade you to spend more than you planned. Learn more about managing your money and personal finances by taking the initiative. Read books, enrol in online courses, or go to workshops on money management. You'll be able to make wise financial decisions and lay a solid basis for your financial future by comprehending ideas like budgeting, credit, and investment.

Budgeting

Let's dive into budgeting. Having a budget is a pretty crucial life skill for both teenagers and adults. Budgeting is all about handling your money sensibly and ensuring that your expenditure is in line with your priorities and goals. You plan how you will spend and save your money when you budget. Plan how much money you have and how much money you need to spend on things. Understanding your income, which is the money you consistently make or receive, is the first step.

This could come from your allowance, side hustles, or any other form of cash you may have. You can begin dividing up your income into various categories as soon as you are aware of how much you have coming in. You may monitor your expenditures and ensure that you aren't overspending in one area at the price of another by allocating specified sums of money to each category. Making deliberate decisions about your spending and where your money goes is made easier with the aid of a budget. Additionally, it enables you to spot spots where you can make cuts if necessary and adapt as necessary to stay on course.

Savings, essentials, entertainment, and objectives are just a few examples of budget categories. Savings are crucial because they enable you to create an emergency fund and accumulate funds for future costs. You require necessities to survive, such as food, clothing, transportation, and any other necessary costs. The term "entertainment" refers to leisure activities like watching films or buying video games. Goals are objectives you desire to accomplish, like saving for a car or making travel plans.

Then, you need to think about what things you need to spend your money on, like clothes or school supplies. You can make a list of these things and how much they cost.

The next step is to keep tabs on your spending. This entails keeping a list of everything you purchase along with its price. To keep track, you can use a notebook or an app on your phone. Since you want to know where your money is going, it's critical to be open and honest about your expenditures. If you are spending too much on one thing, you might need to cut back so you have enough money for other things.

Sticking to your budget

As we discussed in the previous section, spending your money wisely is a key component of adhering to your budget. In order to accomplish the goals you set and have enough money for the things you truly need and want, it's crucial to create a budget and stick to it.

Monitoring your expenditure, as previously stated is one approach to staying under your spending limit. This entails keeping track of the amount of money you spend on various items, such as food, clothing, and gadgets. To keep track of your spending, you can use a journal or an app.

You may keep track of your expenditures and ensure that you aren't overspending in one area at the price of another by allocating specified sums of money to each category. Setting up a budget enables you to prioritise your spending and make thoughtful decisions on your financial priorities. It also enables you to pinpoint areas where you may save money if necessary and make changes to keep on track.

Keep in mind that setting a budget doesn't mean you have to limit your enjoyment of life. It's about being mindful of your finances and ensuring that they are being used in ways that are consistent with your values and objectives. Making the most of your hard-earned money and improving your grasp of your finances are all possible with a careful budget. It's a useful talent that will benefit you all your life.

Making necessary adjustments to your budget is another approach to staying inside it. If you find that you are spending more money than you had anticipated, you might need to make budget cuts elsewhere to make up the difference. As long as you continue to save money and make progress toward your goals, it's acceptable to make changes to your budget.

It's crucial to avoid making impulsive purchases. When you see something you desire, pause to consider whether you actually need it or are just wanting it at the time.

Exercises

Why is it important to track your expenses and create a budget?

What are some common expenses that you may have as a teenager, and how can you effectively manage them within your budget?

How can you differentiate between essential expenses and discretionary expenses when creating your budget?

What are some techniques or tools you can use to stick to your budget and avoid overspending?

How can you adjust your budget when your income or expenses change?

Chapter 5: Financial Goal Setting

By now, you should understand that creating financial goals entails figuring out what you want to do with your money and making a plan to get there. It entails considering your immediate and long-term goals and developing a plan to achieve them.

Setting financial goals enables you to prioritise your needs and direct your resources towards those things. It can involve setting aside money for a certain item you've had your eye on, like a new phone or gaming system. Or it might be setting money aside for experiences like taking a trip with friends or going to a concert. More important long-term objectives, like putting money down for education or beginning your own business, may also be included.

Keep in mind that creating financial goals involves more than just conserving money; it also entails laying the groundwork for future financial security and independence. It gives you the capacity to control your financial situation and make decisions according to your principles and objectives. So have huge dreams, establish high goals, and work to achieve them. You'll be well on your way to realising your dreams and positioning yourself for success if you have the right amount of determination and financial planning.

This has been talked about in the prevoious chapters, however in this chapter we will expand a bit on the topic.

Setting long-term financial goals

A long-term goal is something you intend to accomplish some time in the future, usually over a number of years. It is a goal that must be attained with careful planning, dedication, and persistent effort. Long-term goals usually have a substantial and positive influence on your life, helping to shape its course or improve your general success and well-being.

Examples of long-term goals could include:

Saving for college: Setting a goal to save a certain sum of money over a period of years for college tuition and other costs.

Traveling the world: Saving money and making plans to tour the world to experience other cultures and nations.

Starting a Business: Setting a long-term goal to launch your own company and striving to gather the resources and skills required.

Career Advancement: Setting goals to seek higher education, acquire particular abilities, or obtain internships in order to advance in your selected job field.

Buying a home: Planning to save money for a down payment on a home or apartment that you hope to buy in the future.

Retirement planning: Setting a long-term goal to regularly contribute to a retirement savings account in order to assure your financial security in your later years.

To be accomplished, these goals need constant dedication over time. They could entail budgeting, acquiring knowledge or skills, establishing networks, and making calculated choices to get you closer to your goals. Setting long-term goals will help you map out your future, stay motivated, and make decisions that are in line with your dreams.

To set long-term financial goals effectively, break them down into smaller, manageable steps. This approach allows you to track your progress and stay motivated along the way. For instance, if your goal is to save money for college, you can set smaller milestones like saving a certain amount each month or finding ways to increase your income through part-time jobs or scholarships.

It's also crucial to consider the time horizon of your goals. Long-term goals require more time and commitment, so it's important to be patient and persistent.

Creating a plan to achieve them

A critical first step in reaching your financial goals for the future is planning. As you work towards your goal, it enables you to stay motivated, organised, and focused. To make a plan to accomplish your long-term goals, follow these steps:

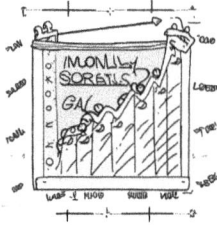

Set Specific Goals: Clearly define and list your long-term objectives. Set a deadline for completing your goals and be clear about what you hope to achieve.

Divide It Up: Your long-term objective should be broken down into manageable pieces. Your goal should be broken down into manageable monthly, quarterly, or annual goals.

Set achievable goals: Decide how much cash, resources, or milestones you need to reach at each stage. Be honest with yourself about what you can achieve given the time and resources you have available.

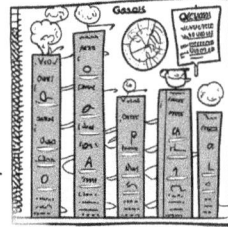

Create a budget: Create a budget that supports your long-term objectives. Set aside money for your goals, making sure you have enough to progress while still paying for other obligations. *See Chapter 4 for more.*

Track your progress: Keep track of how far you've come toward your long-term objectives. Keep a record of the money you save, the investments you make, and any other steps you take to achieve your goals.

Adjust as required: Regularly review your plan and, if required, make improvements. You might need to update your plan to new chances or problems if your life circumstances change.

Seek support and guidance: Think about getting assistance from mentors, trusted adults, or financial experts who can help you reach your goals.

Keep in mind that making a plan is only the first step. Along the journey, it's critical to retain consistency, discipline, and motivation. Celebrate your achievements and advancements to maintain your drive. You may make significant progress towards accomplishing your long-term financial goals if you have a clear plan and a strong dedication to it.

Exercises

1. Why is it important to set financial goals?
2. What are some short-term and long-term financial goals you have for yourself?
3. How can you break down your goals into smaller, achievable steps?
4. What are some strategies you can use to stay motivated and focused on reaching your financial goals?
5. How can you measure your progress towards your financial goals and make adjustments along the way?

Chapter 6: Credit Scores & Reports

The ability to borrow money or to purchase goods and services with the promise to pay for them later is referred to as having **credit**. It is a financial arrangement in which a lender or creditor lends you money or permits you to make a purchase with the understanding that you will pay the money back over a predetermined period, typically with interest.

Different sorts of credit are possible. One typical type is a loan, when you agree to borrow a certain sum of money from a bank or other lending organisation and repay it over time in installments. A credit card is another option, which enables you to make purchases up to a predetermined credit limit and pay back the balance in full or with just the minimum in monthly installments.

Access to credit can be useful in a variety of circumstances. It enables you to make purchases when you don't have access to cash right away, like when buying a car, paying for college, or handling unforeseen costs. Additionally, it can aid in establishing a credit history, which is crucial for future financial activities like applying for loans, renting an apartment, or even finding employment.

It's crucial to utilise credit properly, though. When you borrow money or use credit, you are assuming financial responsibility, thus it's important to use credit responsibly. This entails paying your bills on time, managing your debt, and being aware of the interest rates and other costs related to using credit. You may establish a good credit history and keep a secure financial future by utilising credit sensibly.

Understanding credit scores

Teenagers who are just starting to learn about personal finance should understand credit scores. Your creditworthiness, that is your ability to repay, depends on your credit score, which shows how likely you are to pay back loans. Lenders, renters, and even prospective employers use it to determine your level of financial responsibility.

Your payment history, the total amount of debt you owe, the length of your credit history, and the types of credit you have are just a few of the factors that affect your credit score. Compared to a borrower with a lower credit score, you have a higher credit score if you have a good credit history and are viewed as a lower risk borrower.

Good credit is necessary since it makes it possible to secure loans, rent an apartment, or even get credit cards with low interest rates. Pay your bills on time, keep your credit utilisation low, and refrain from taking on excessive debt if you want to keep or raise your credit score.

It's a good idea to check your credit report frequently. It gives you a thorough account of your credit history and aides in finding any mistakes or inconsistencies that might have an effect on your credit score. Teenagers may position themselves for financial success and future possibilities by understanding credit ratings and trying to develop a favourable credit history.

Maintaining a good credit score

For the sake of your finances, it is crucial to maintain a high credit score. A three-digit number called your credit score indicates your creditworthiness and aids lenders in determining the risk of lending you money. A high credit score shows that you have been a responsible consumer of money, which might make it simpler for you to get loans, credit cards, or lower interest rates. To maintain a good credit score, it's important to follow these practices:

Maintain a low credit utilisation rate: Credit utilisation is the percentage of your available credit that is being used at any one time. Keep your credit use below 30%, as advised. High credit utilisation can lower your credit score because it indicates that you heavily rely on credit.

Pay your bills on time: It's important to meet all of your financial commitments, including loan payments and credit card bills, on time. Your credit score may be negatively impacted by late payments.

Limit the number of new accounts: Opening many credit accounts quickly can raise questions about your stability. It's best to keep a manageable amount of accounts and only apply for new credit when absolutely essential.

Be careful when closing credit accounts because doing so can have an impact on your credit score by shortening your credit history and increasing your credit utilisation ratio. Before cancelling any accounts, take the potential effects into mind.

Monitor your credit report for any inaccuracies, fraudulent activity, or anomalies on a regular basis. To preserve an accurate credit history, errors must be reported and swiftly resolved.

Create a wide credit mix: Having a variety of credit, including installment loans, credit cards, and a mortgage, will help your credit score. It's important to only accept credit, though, that you can handle responsibly.

Consequences of a low score

Difficulty obtaining loans: A low credit score can make it difficult to qualify for loans in the future, including student loans and auto loans. You could be considered a greater risk borrower by lenders, in which case they might reject your loan application or present you with less enticing terms, including higher interest rates.

Limited access to credit: Applying for credit cards or other lines of credit can be more difficult if you have a poor credit score. Even if you are accepted, the credit limit can be lower, which would make it harder to pay for bigger purchases or unplanned bills.

Higher interest rates: If you're able to get a loan or credit despite having a low credit score, you may have to pay interest rates that are much higher. This implies that you'll have to pay more interest over time, which may increase your expenses and possibly make it more difficult to pay off your debts.

Teenagers who are aware of these implications may be encouraged to take charge of enhancing and maintaining their credit scores. You can position yourself for a more secure financial future by developing sound financial practices at a young age, such as paying bills on time and using credit responsibly.

Exercises

1. What is a credit score and why is it important?
2. How can you maintain a good credit score and what factors can impact it?
3. What are some potential consequences of having a low credit score?
4. How can you access and review your credit report?
5. What are some strategies you can use to build and improve your credit history as a teenager?

Chapter 7: Entrepreneurship

The process of beginning and operating a business or endeavour with the intention of turning a profit is known as **entrepreneurship**. To produce and deliver goods or services to clients, entails seeing opportunities, taking calculated risks, and making use of available resources. Entrepreneurs are those with a distinct vision, creativity, and motivation to realise their ideas.

Innovation is a crucial component of entrepreneurship. Entrepreneurs frequently look for novel and creative ways to solve issues or satisfy market demands. They are prepared to take chances and put money, time, and effort into their business ventures in the hopes of being prosperous and financially independent.

Other tasks associated with entrepreneurship include planning, budgeting, marketing, and running a company's day-to-day operations. To expand and sustain their enterprises, entrepreneurs must identify their target market, create a business plan, get capital or investment, sell their goods or services, and make wise judgements.

Through entrepreneurship, people may follow their passions, express their creativity, and take charge of their own destiny. It can result in financial independence, personal fulfilment, and the capacity to improve society by fostering job creation and economic growth.

In general, being an entrepreneur involves taking the initiative, accepting obstacles, and taking advantage of opportunities to convert ideas into profitable businesses. Vision, tenacity, adaptability, and a strong entrepreneurial mindset are all necessary.

Business plans

A business plan is a written document that covers the objectives, plans, and day-to-day operations of a company. It acts as the organization's road map, giving it a clear course and foundation for success. Entrepreneurs can express their vision to potential investors, partners, and stakeholders by using a well-written business plan.

Several important elements are often included in a business plan. In the beginning, it offers an executive summary that gives a general overview of the company, its objective, and the issue it seeks to address. To show the economic potential and future success of the business, it also comprises a thorough description of the supplied goods or services, a target market study, and a competition analysis.

A business plan also describes the management team, key employees, and organisational structure of the company. It outlines the price, promotion, and distribution tactics as well as the marketing and sales strategies. It also contains a thorough financial analysis that forecasts revenues, costs, and profitability over a given time period.

Because they offer an organised method to starting and running a business, business plans are essential. They support business owners by assisting them with problem-solving, decision-making, and raising capital. An effective business plan serves as a road map for achievement and can be updated as the company grows.

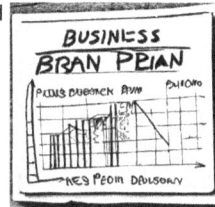

In the end, a business plan functions as a strategic instrument that enables entrepreneurs to define their goals, create a plan of action, and improve the likelihood that they will succeed.

Marketing strategies

The process of beginning and operating a business or endeavour with the intention of turning a profit is known as entrepreneurship. To produce and deliver goods or services to clients, it entails seeing opportunities, taking calculated risks, and making use of available resources. Entrepreneurs are those with a distinct vision, creativity, and motivation to realise their ideas.

Advertising is a popular marketing approach that involves developing engaging messages or pictures to promote the benefits and qualities of a product or service. This can be accomplished through a variety of means, including television, social media, and print media. Teenagers can experiment with several channels to promote their projects or ideas, such as social media, personal websites, or local community boards.

Branding is another marketing approach that involves developing a unique identity for a product, service, or personal brand. This includes creating a logo, tagline, and visual components that set the offering apart from competitors. Teenagers might evaluate how they want to exhibit themselves or their ideas to others, taking into account elements such as their target audience, values, and the image they wish to project.

Social media marketing is another popular method, particularly among teens who are quite active on internet platforms. This entails connecting with and engaging a specific audience using social media sites. Teens can use these platforms to promote their ideas, showcase their talents, and create a community centred on their interests.

Finally, word-of-mouth marketing is a technique that is based on favourable recommendations and referrals from happy consumers. By offering exceptional experiences, developing shareable material, and actively connecting with their audience, teenagers can urge others to spread the news about their projects or activities.

Understanding marketing methods as a teenager gives you the ability to effectively express your ideas, establish an audience, and achieve your objectives. You can build skills that can help you in many aspects of your life by learning about diverse marketing methods, whether it's promoting personal projects, organising events, or exploring business prospects.

Taxes

Taxes are payments made to the government and are an important component of how the government pays public services and programmes. As a teen, you may have overheard your parents or other adults discussing taxes, but what precisely are they?

When you earn money from a job, whether through part-time work or otherwise, you must normally pay taxes on it. These taxes are used by the government to pay things like schools, hospitals, roads, and public safety. It's a means for everyone in the community to contribute their fair part to the services and infrastructure that we all rely on.

There are various forms of taxes, including income tax, sales tax, and property tax. If you have a regular job, income tax is normally deducted directly from your paycheck. Sales tax is a modest percentage applied to the price of products and services such as clothing and video games. Homeowners pay property tax based on the value of their home.

Understanding taxes is essential for becoming responsible citizens. By paying taxes, we contribute to the well-being of our community and help ensure that everyone has access to critical services. It is also critical to maintain track of your income and expenses in order to appropriately report your taxes and meet your legal duties.

Exercises

1. What is entrepreneurship and why is it an important skill to develop?
2. What are some examples of successful teenage entrepreneurs and their businesses?
3. How can you identify a business idea that aligns with your interests and skills?
4. What are some steps you can take to start your own small business as a teenager?
5. What are some challenges and rewards you may experience as an entrepreneur, and how can you overcome obstacles along the way?

Chapter 8: Insurance

Insurance protects you and your things against unforeseeable disasters or accidents. It acts as a safety net, allowing you to recoup financially if something goes wrong. When you get insurance, you pay a set amount of money to an insurance company known as a premium. In exchange, the insurance company guarantees to assist you financially if something unfortunate occurs.

Insurance comes in many forms, including health insurance, auto insurance, and house insurance. If you get sick or injured, health insurance can assist cover the cost of your medical bills. Auto insurance protects you in the event of a car accident and assists in the payment of any damages or injuries. Home insurance protects you if your house is damaged by a fire, storm, or other natural disaster.

Having insurance gives you peace of mind since you know that if something unforeseen occurs, you will not carry the entire financial load. It can assist you in avoiding huge bills that you may be unable to afford on your own. Insurance is especially crucial for items that are valuable or necessary to you, such as your health, automobile, or home.

It is critical to understand the terms and conditions of your insurance policy, as well as what is and is not covered. You should also pay your insurance premiums on time in order to maintain your coverage valid. While insurance is a financial commitment, it can bring peace of mind and protect you against major financial disasters in the future.

Types of insurance

When you get sick or injured, **health insurance** can assist cover your medical expenses. Doctor appointments, hospital stays, prescription prescriptions, and preventive care are all examples of what it can encompass. Health insurance ensures that you can obtain vital healthcare treatments without incurring substantial financial costs. Depending on your country's healthcare system, it can be obtained through private providers or government programmes.

Auto insurance is specifically designed to safeguard you and your vehicle in the event of an accident or damage. It covers vehicle damage, injuries to yourself or others, and liability for property damage caused by your vehicle. Auto insurance is required in most states and helps to lessen the financial effects of car accidents, repairs, and medical expenditures.

Home insurance protects your home and its belongings against a variety of threats. It provides coverage for losses caused by fire, theft, vandalism, natural catastrophes, and other unforeseeable incidents. Home insurance often covers the construction of your home, personal items, and liabilities in the event that someone is injured on your property. It provides you peace of knowing that if something happens to your home, you are financially insured.

These are just a few examples of the numerous insurance alternatives available. Life insurance, disability insurance, renters insurance, and more sorts are also available. Each type serves a distinct purpose in assisting individuals and families in managing the financial risks connected with various elements of their lives. It is critical to understand the coverage, terms, and conditions of your insurance plans in order to ensure that you have adequate protection for your needs.

How it works

Insurance works by distributing the risk of potential financial losses over a wide number of people. When you buy an insurance policy, you enter into a contract with the insurance provider. The insurance business commits to offer financial protection and reimbursement in exchange for monthly premium payments.This is how insurance usually works:

Policy acquisition: You select the sort of insurance you require and a policy from an insurance provider. The policy details the coverage, terms, and conditions, as well as the premium amount you must pay.

Payment of premiums: To keep your coverage, you must pay the insurance company on a regular basis. Depending on the insurance terms, these premiums can be paid monthly, quarterly, or annually.

Coverage period: The insurance policy specifies the time period in which you are covered. If an insured incident occurs during this time period, you may file a claim for compensation.

Insured event: If you have a covered occurrence, such as an accident, illness, theft, or property damage, you must tell your insurance company and file a claim. Specific paperwork and information about the incident will be required for the claim.

Claim evaluation: The insurance company examines your claim to see if it is valid and covered by the policy. They may ask for further information or evidence to back up your claim.

Compensation: If your claim is accepted, the insurance company will pay you according to the terms of your policy. Depending on the nature of the claim, this could take the form of reimbursement, repairs, replacement, or direct cash.

Deductibles and limits: Some insurance policies require you to pay a deductible, which is the amount of money you must pay out of pocket before the insurance coverage kicks in. Policy limitations determine the maximum amount that an insurance company will pay for a claim.

Policy renewal: Insurance policies are normally good for a set amount of time, such as a year. You can choose to renew the policy by continuing to pay premiums at the end of the coverage period.

Individuals and their assets are protected against financial loss by insurance. To ensure you have the correct protection for your needs, carefully check and understand the terms and conditions of your insurance policy, including coverage, exclusions, and claim procedures.

Exercises

1. What is insurance and why is it important to have insurance coverage?
2. What are some common types of insurance, such as health, auto, and home insurance?
3. How can insurance help protect you from financial risks and unexpected events?
4. What factors should you consider when choosing insurance coverage that best suits your needs?
5. How can you be a responsible insurance policyholder and effectively manage your insurance premiums and claims?

Chapter 9: Financial Responsibility

Financial responsibility is the ability to make informed and responsible financial decisions and manage your financial resources successfully. Understanding and practising healthy financial habits, being accountable for your financial activities, and taking charge of your financial well-being are all part of the process.

Financial responsibility entails living within your means and making deliberate decisions about how you earn, spend, save, and invest your money. To guarantee that your income is wisely allocated and used to fulfill your requirements, wants, and long-term financial objectives, rigorous budgeting, and planning are required.

Financial responsibility also includes debt management. This includes not getting into too much debt, paying your bills on time, and understanding the terms and conditions of any loans or credit agreements you have. To avoid financial difficulty, it is necessary to make informed judgments regarding borrowing money and using credit cards properly.

Furthermore, financial responsibility entails planning for the future by saving and investing. It entails putting money aside for emergencies, saving for short- and long-term goals, and thinking about investment opportunities that can help you expand your wealth over time. (*See chapters 3-5*).

Overall, being financially responsible gives you more control over your financial status, allows you to make good financial decisions, and works towards financial stability and success. It is a valuable talent that can improve many parts of your life and pave the road for a safe and prosperous future.

Importance of financial responsibility

Financial stability: Financial responsibility entails planning for the future by saving and investing. It entails putting money aside for emergencies, saving for short- and long-term goals, and thinking about investment opportunities that can help you expand your wealth over time.

Goal achievement: Being financially responsible gives you more control over your financial status, allows you to make good financial decisions, and works towards financial stability and success. It is a valuable talent that can improve many parts of your life and pave the road for a safe and prosperous future.

Debt management: Financial responsibility is essential for efficient debt management. You may prevent debt from spiraling out of control by making timely payments, avoiding excessive borrowing, and knowing the terms and circumstances of loans or credit agreements. This not only safeguards your credit score but also guarantees you the financial flexibility to pursue other goals and opportunities.

Emergency preparedness: Life is unpredictable, and unexpected expenses can occur at any time. By exercising financial discipline, you can save for unexpected events such as medical emergencies, car repairs, or job loss. Having emergency reserves on hand creates a sense of security and lessens the temptation to use credit or accumulate high-interest debt.

Future Financial Freedom: Financial responsibility lays the groundwork for future financial freedom and independence. You can develop wealth over time and create a solid financial foundation for your future by saving and investing sensibly. Responsible financial habits also help you establish solid money management abilities that will serve you well throughout your life, allowing you to make informed decisions and effectively navigate financial obstacles.

Furthemore, financial responsibility is critical for achieving financial well-being, accomplishing goals, and living a satisfying life. It gives you the tools and skills you need to make good financial decisions, adapt to changing circumstances, and build a prosperous financial future.

Risks of overspending

Overspending is defined as spending more money than you have or going above what you can afford. While it may be tempting to seek immediate gratification and buy what you want, there are various hazards involved with overspending that might have long-term negative implications, such as;

Financial Instability: Excessive spending can cause financial stress and instability. When you continually spend more money than you earn, you may find yourself unable to pay your expenses, incurring debt, and living paycheck to paycheck. Anxiety, sleepless nights, and continual worry about how to make ends meet can result from financial stress. It can also make it difficult to save for the future or deal with unexpected bills.

Debt Accumulation: Overspending frequently results in building up debt, especially if you rely largely on credit cards or loans to fuel your spending habits. High-interest debt can quickly accumulate, making it difficult to pay off obligations and even locking you in a debt cycle. The more debt you have, the more interest you must pay, which can have a substantial influence on your financial well-being and limit your future financial alternatives.

Impaired Financial Goals: Excessive spending might make it difficult to meet essential financial goals. Excessive spending takes money away from goals like saving for a house, supporting your school, or building an emergency fund. Your financial resources are diverted to short-term pleasures, making it more difficult to achieve long-term financial security and pursue your dreams. Overspending might slow your progress towards financial independence and limit your future options.

Lack of Financial Freedom: Excessive spending might limit your financial freedom and limit your options. If you routinely overspend, you may find yourself locked in a loop of working longer hours or taking on other jobs to make ends meet. This can result in a lack of flexibility and the inability to pursue your interests or make decisions based on what is actually important to you.

Another factor to consider is the fact that, you may not be able to pay your bills due to overspending. This may lead to certain services and access you have being revoked by the provider.

Recognising the risks of overspending and developing healthy financial habits are critical. Self-discipline, budgeting, and discriminating between necessities and wants can help you avoid the traps of overspending and strive towards a more secure and happier financial future.

Importance of saving for emergencies

Saving for emergencies is important for various reasons, including financial security and peace of mind in the event of an emergency:

Financial security: Life is full of unknowns, and emergencies can occur at any time. It could be an unexpected medical bill, car repairs, or job loss. Having an emergency fund allows you to deal with these unforeseen costs without having to take out high-interest loans or incur debt. Setting money away, particularly for emergencies creates a financial safety net that can help you handle difficult times with greater ease while minimising the impact on your overall financial well-being.

Avoiding Debt: Without an emergency fund, people frequently borrow money to cover unforeseen bills. This might result in debt that takes time and effort to repay. High interest rates on loans or credit cards can quickly mount up, making financial recovery difficult. By setting aside money for emergencies, you can avoid having to use credit and maintain your financial security.

Peace of Mind and Reduced Stress: Knowing that you have money set up for emergencies gives you peace of mind and decreases financial stress. It gives you peace of mind that you have something to fall back on if anything unexpected happens. This peace of mind allows you to concentrate on other elements of your life, such as work, family, and personal objectives, without being concerned about how you would face a financial catastrophe. Having emergency savings allows you to confront challenges with confidence, knowing that you are prepared to deal with unforeseen occurrences.

Creating an emergency fund necessitates persistent savings over time. As a general rule, aim to save three to six months' worth of living expenses. You may develop a financial cushion that provides protection, reduces the need for debt, and brings peace of mind at unexpected times by making regular contributions to your emergency fund and keeping it distinct from your day-to-day expenditures.

Creating an emergency fund necessitates persistent savings over time. As a general rule, aim to save three to six months' worth of living expenses. You may develop a financial cushion that provides protection, reduces the need for debt, and brings peace of mind at unexpected times by making regular contributions to your emergency fund and keeping it distinct from your day-to-day expenditures.

Exercises

1. What does it mean to be financially responsible?
2. Why is it important to pay bills on time and manage your debts responsibly?
3. How can you practice responsible borrowing and avoid accumulating excessive debt?
4. What are some strategies you can use to save money for emergencies and unexpected expenses?
5. How can you make informed decisions when considering major financial commitments, such as buying a car or renting an apartment?

Chapter 10: Careers & Income

A career is a person's chosen profession or occupation that they pursue for an extended length of time. It entails engaging in a certain area of work, which frequently necessitates specific skills, expertise, education, and training. A career is often connected with long-term employment in a certain field or business that provides opportunity for progress, growth, and professional development. While income refers to the money earned through employment or other sources.

Choosing a job entails taking into account one's interests, passions, abilities, and ambitions in order to discover a path that matches with one's aspirations and values. It necessitates deliberate decision-making, self-reflection, and investigation of numerous job choices. Careers can be found in a variety of industries and sectors, including healthcare, technology, education, business, arts and entertainment, and many others.

A successful profession frequently entails ongoing learning and skill development in order to adapt to changing demands and improvements in one's chosen area. It could entail furthering one's education, obtaining certificates, or gaining practical experience through internships or apprenticeships. Many people advance in their careers by moving through several stages, taking on greater responsibilities, and seeking new challenges and possibilities.

A successful career can provide a sense of purpose, personal happiness, and accomplishment in addition to a source of cash. It enables individuals to put their skills to use, contribute to society, and make a significant difference in their chosen sector. Career choices can influence a person's lifestyle and financial security, as well as play a big effect in their general well-being and happiness.

Different types of jobs

Healthcare Jobs: Doctors, nurses, pharmacists, medical technicians, therapists, and other healthcare professionals labour to offer medical care and support to those in need.

Technology Jobs: include software developers, computer programmers, data analysts, network administrators, and cybersecurity specialists, to name a few.

Education Jobs: Teachers, academics, school administrators, tutors, and educational counsellors all play important roles in developing students' minds and providing them with knowledge and direction.

Business Jobs: In the business world, business managers, marketers, sales representatives, accountants, human resource experts, and entrepreneurs oversee operations, promote products or services, manage funds, and encourage growth.

Creative Jobs: Artists, writers, musicians, actors, designers, photographers, and filmmakers work in the creative industries, putting their skills to use to create artistic and entertaining works.

Trades Jobs: Plumbers, electricians, carpenters, mechanics, and construction workers are trained professionals who work with their hands, providing important services connected to infrastructure creation, repair, and maintenance.

Service Industry: Waiters/waitresses, baristas, retail employees, customer service representatives, and hospitality staff serve and assist clients in restaurants, cafes, stores, hotels, and other service-oriented situations.

Government jobs: Police officers, firefighters, civil employees, diplomats, and politicians work in government to enforce laws, provide public services, represent constituents, and rule a country or region.

How to prepare for them

Education and Skills: Research the educational requirements and essential skills for the job path you want to pursue. Determine whether a college diploma, vocational training, or specialised certifications are required. Concentrate on gaining appropriate skills and information for your chosen field through courses, internships, or extracurricular activities.

Exploration and Self-Assessment: Take the time to investigate other job paths and evaluate your interests, talents, and values. Determine what you enjoy doing and what corresponds with your long-term objectives. To get personal knowledge, consider interacting with professionals in your intended field, attending career fairs, or participating in job shadowing opportunities.

Establish clear and attainable goals to steer your work development. These objectives may include obtaining a specified level of schooling, having work experience in a suitable field, or learning specific skills. To stay motivated and on track, break down your goals into smaller, more doable tasks.

Networking: Connect with people in your target field to build a network of professional contacts. To make significant relationships, attend business events, join professional organisations, and use internet platforms like LinkedIn. Mentorship, employment referrals, and industry insights can all be obtained through networking.

Gain Experience: Look for internships, part-time work, or volunteer opportunities that will provide you with hands-on experience in your field of interest. This hands-on experience not only boosts your résumé, but it also gives you crucial insights into the realities of the profession and allows you to build applicable abilities.

Continuous Learning: Using continuous learning, you may stay up to speed on industry trends, innovations, and new technology. To stay competitive in the employment market, take use of online courses, workshops, webinars, or professional development programmes.

Professional Growth: Develop strong interpersonal skills, good communication skills, and problem-solving ability. Concentrate on honing your leadership potential, flexibility, and teamwork abilities, as these are highly desired in any profession.

How to excel at your job

Set clear, quantifiable Goals: Establish clear, quantifiable goals that match with your job responsibilities and your organization's broader objectives. Having specific goals gives you focus and direction, allowing you to prioritise tasks and strive towards reaching exceptional results.

Take Initiative: Be proactive and take charge of your work. Look for ways to go above and beyond your allotted tasks by taking on more responsibility, recommending changes, and coming up with creative solutions to problems. Demonstrate passion for new challenges and a willingness to learn new skills.

Develop Your Skills: Consistently build and improve your job-related talents. Keep abreast of industry trends and breakthroughs, and look for learning opportunities such as workshops, training programmes, and online courses. Developing a diverse skill set will not only make you more productive in your current work but will also provide prospects for advancement.

Communicate Effectively: Effective communication is essential for job success. Communicate information clearly and simply, actively listen to others, and seek clarification when necessary. Develop good written and oral communication skills to ensure that your ideas are received and that you can effectively cooperate with colleagues and clients.

Collaboration and Relationship Building: Develop strong working relationships with your coworkers, superiors, and clients. Collaborate efficiently with people while respecting different points of view and emphasising cooperation. Seek opportunities to contribute to team efforts, assist colleagues, and share your knowledge. Building solid professional relationships not only improves the work environment but also provides opportunities for networking and career progress.

Maintain Professionalism: Show professionalism in all parts of your work. Be on time, meet deadlines, and produce high-quality work. Accept accountability for your acts, accept your mistakes, and learn from them. Maintain your integrity, honesty, and respect for others, and keep a cheerful attitude even in difficult situations.

Exercises

1. What is the importance of exploring different career options and understanding your interests and skills?
2. How can you prepare for a successful career by acquiring the necessary education and skills?
3. What are some strategies you can use to stand out during job interviews and make a positive impression on potential employers?
4. How can you negotiate a fair salary and benefits package when starting a new job?
5. What are some ways you can continue to grow and advance in your chosen career field?

www.ingramcontent.com/pod-product-compliance
Lightning Source LLC
Chambersburg PA
CBHW021944040426
42448CB00008B/1239